Table of Contents

Introduction

Thanks for downloading this book. Now you will discover at least three basic massage techniques in the comfort of your home and easily develop a closer relationship with your family and friends!

You are serious about wanting to be the "go to" person with those "magical hands" since you have downloaded "Massage Therapy - Massage Therapy Techniques - How to Give a Soothing Massage from Head to Toe".

In this fully illustrated picture book with over 50 photos you will discover step by step:

- How to effectively give a relaxing back massage to relieve muscle soreness
- How to effectively give a soothing neck massage to relieve muscle pain
- How to effectively give a shoulder massage to relieve muscle tightness
- How to effectively give a relaxation massage
- How to effectively relieve a pain in the "butt" from sitting at a computer all day!

What are you waiting for?

Get started now!

Warmest regards

Mike

Affiliate Compensation Disclosure

Please note this eBook contains hyperlinks to other books, individuals or websites.

The author does not have any control over third party terms and policies. You click on these links at your own risk.

These links may lead to the other resources from the author or researched and tried products in which there has been a positive influence.

The links provided are done so in good faith.

You understand that you still need to do your own due diligence and decide what is best with you.

YOU MUST ALWAYS DO YOUR DUE DILLIGENCE WHEN PURCHASING OVER THE INTERNET!

THIS INCLUDES PURCHASING THROUGH AFFILIATE LINKS.

Effleurage

Effleurage is an introductory stroke usually with light pressure to introduce your partner to your touch.

It also helps to get the oil on. You start and finish your massage with this technique.

Start at shoulders and work your way down the back.

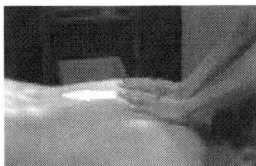

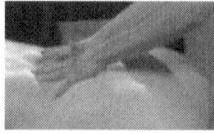

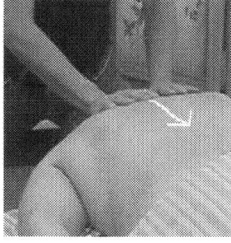

MASSAGE THERAPY
Basic Massage Techniques

discover how to give
a soothing massage
from head to toe

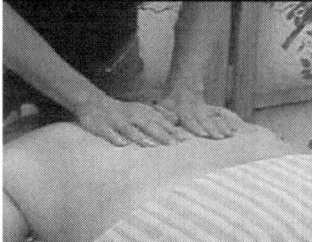

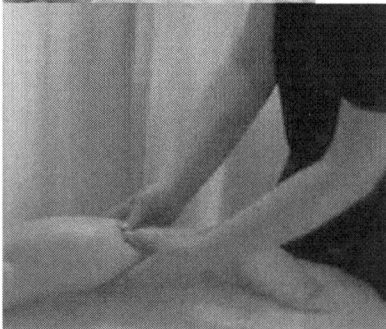

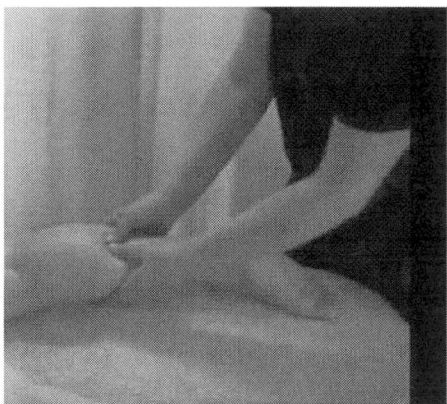

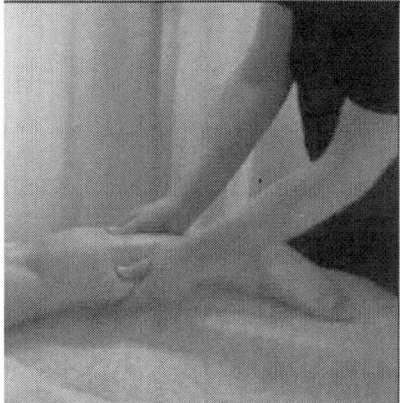

Start at shoulders and work your down the arms.

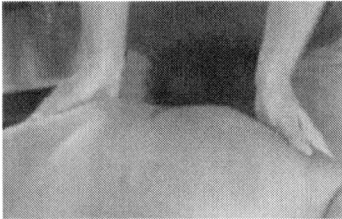

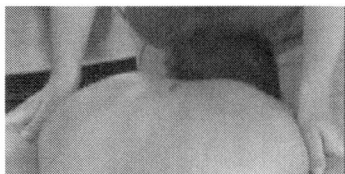

Start at low back and work to shoulders then down the side of the body. Repeat

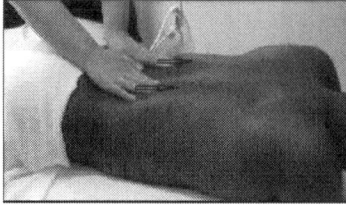

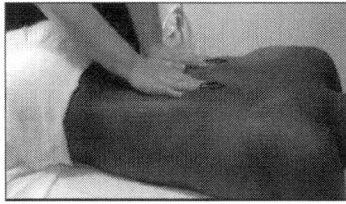

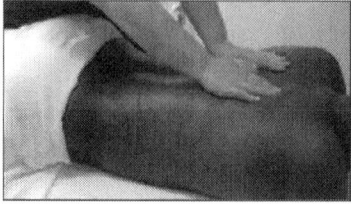

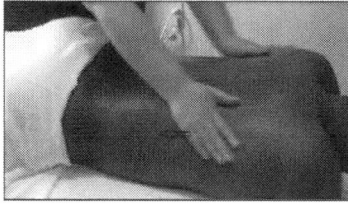

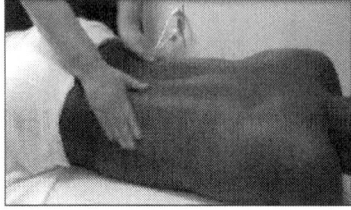

Shingling

This is a simple technique in which one hand follows the other on the same side of the body. Light pressure is used.

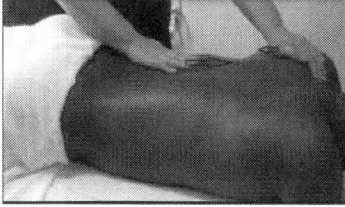

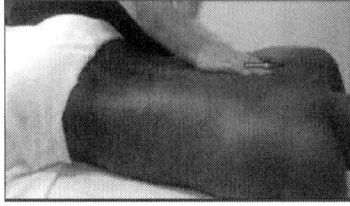

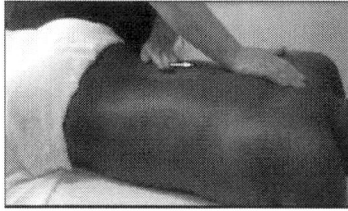

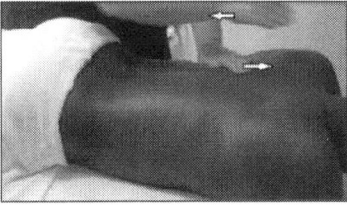

Kneading

Think about kneading dough with your hands. You squeezing, lifting up and doing movements in a circular fashion or a straight forward motion.

This pressure may start light but can always go deeper with pressure.

Finger Tip Kneading

The focus is pressure from the finger tips

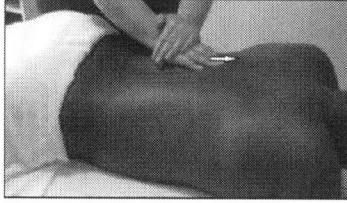

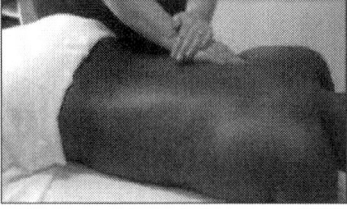

Thumb Kneading

The pressure is from the palmar side of the thumb.

Calf muscle –thumbs together then spread out.

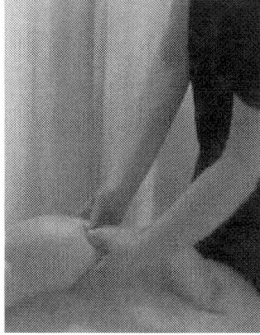

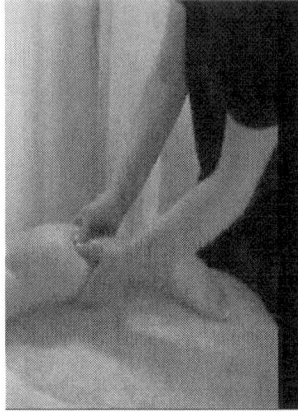

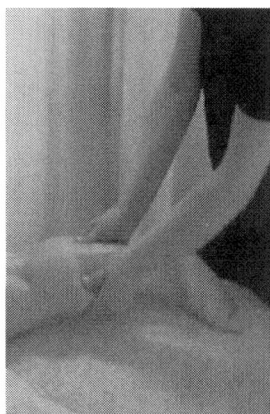

Thumb Kneading for the Back

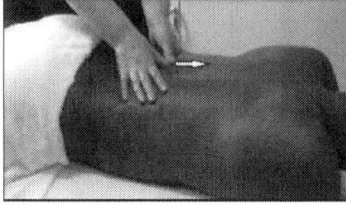

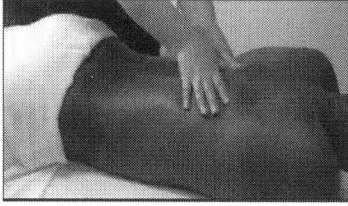

Reinforced Palmar Kneading

The pressure is from the palm

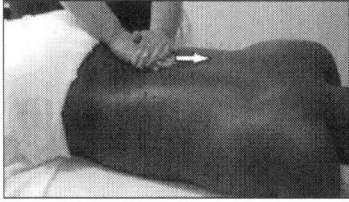

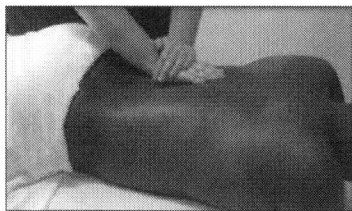

Wringing

This technique is like wringing a wet towel to dry it. Only here you are doing this on the body.

In the examples below it is showing it on the back.

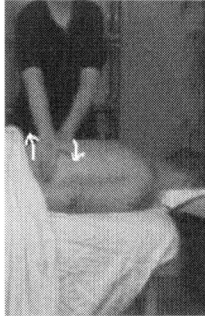

MASSAGE THERAPY
Basic Massage Techniques

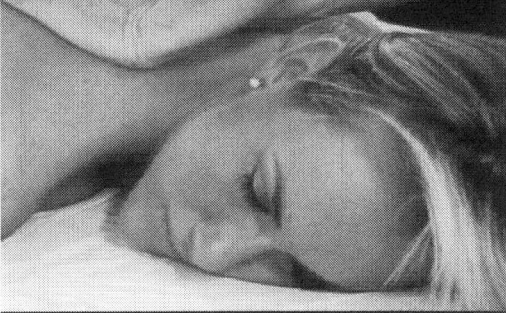

discover how to give
a soothing massage
from head to toe

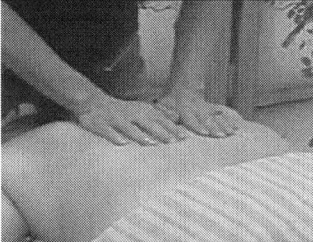

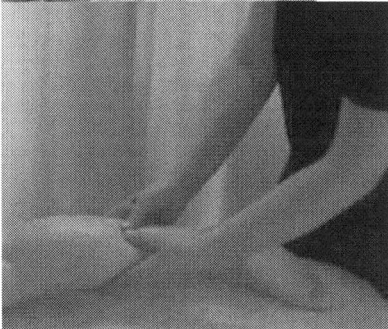

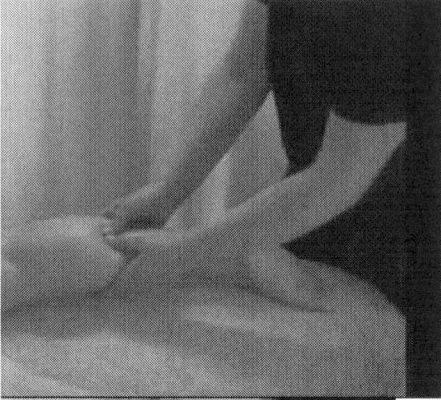
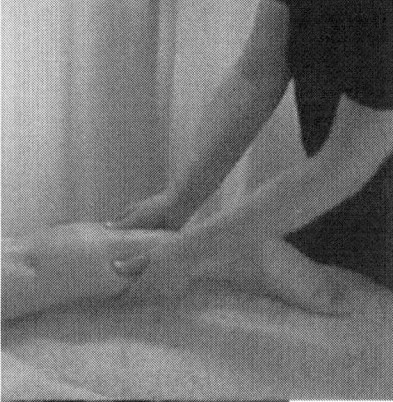
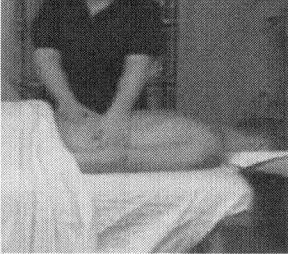

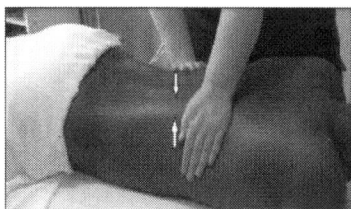

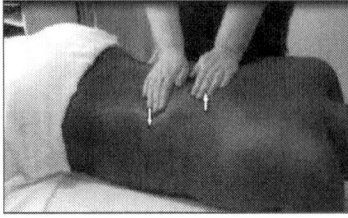

MASSAGE THERAPY
Basic Massage Techniques

discover how to give
a soothing massage
from head to toe

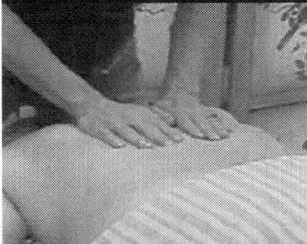

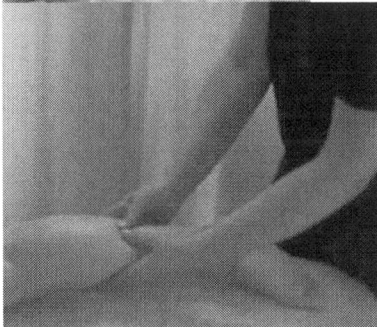

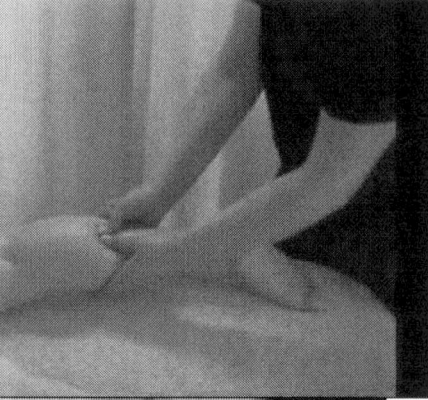

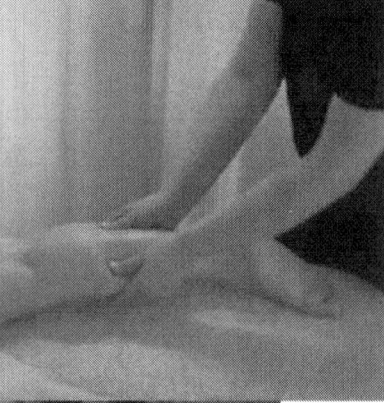

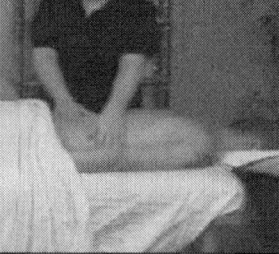

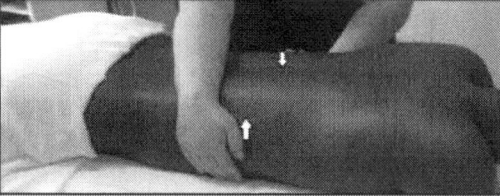

Percussive Techniques

Think of these techniques as playing the drums with different parts of your hand.

Pincement

Think of quickly alternating pinching the skin quickly while tapping at the same time.

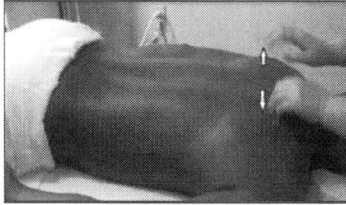

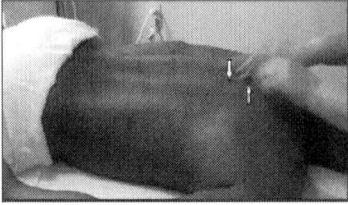

Cupping

Think of putting your hand out in front of as if to scoop water into them and then drink from them.

Now for the hand position for this technique turn your hands so your palms face down put stay in a "cupped" position.

Alternate the hands

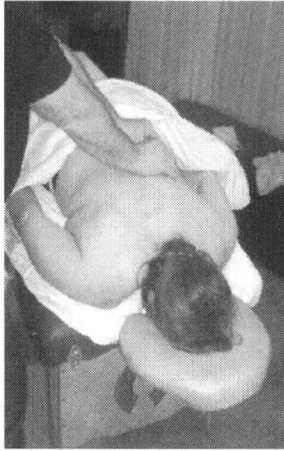

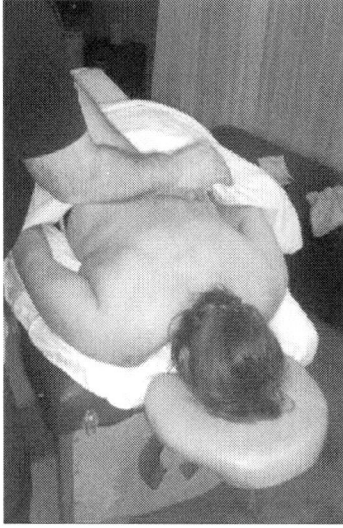

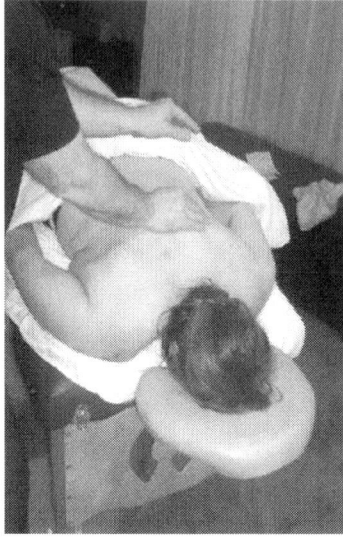

Pounding

Think of pounding a door. Your hand is in a clinched position as those you are going to punch something.

Except in this technique it is the side surface of the "pinky" finger that makes contact with the skin.

This technique is mainly used in areas of lots of tissue.

The most common area is the glues /buttock area.

Alternate Hands

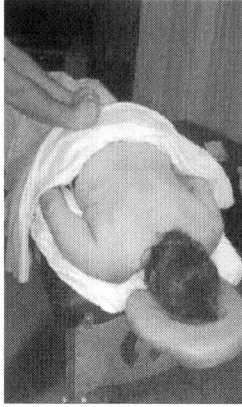

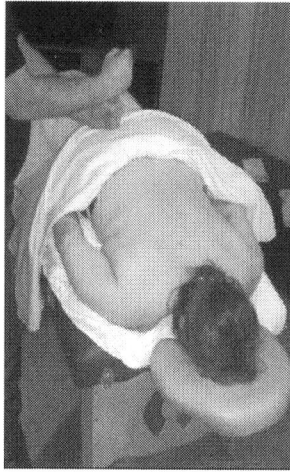

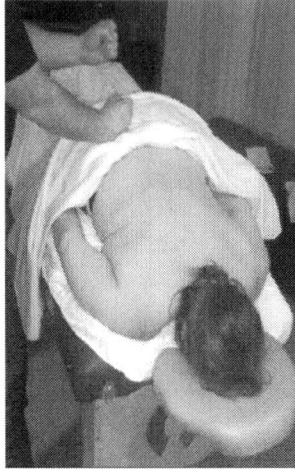

Hacking

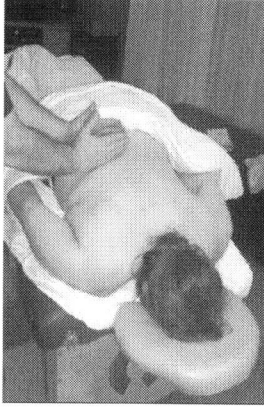

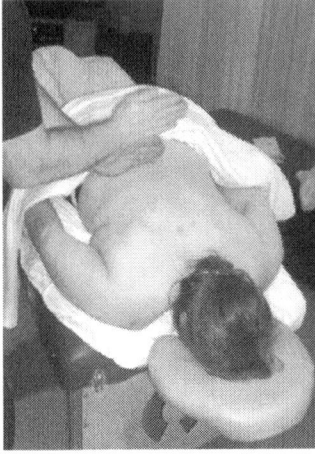

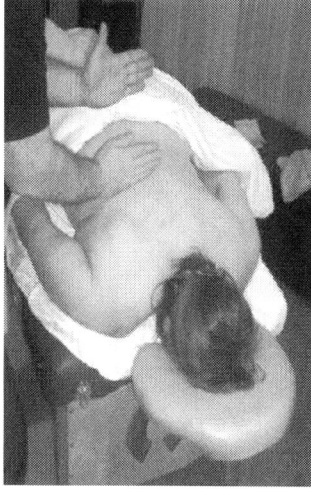

Abdominal Massage

This is a circular motion. You may also use the <u>effleurage</u> technique as well

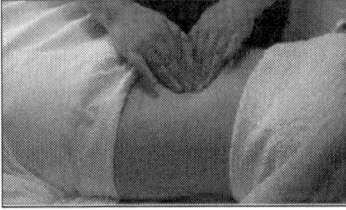

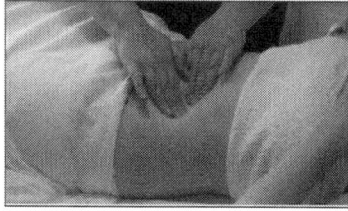

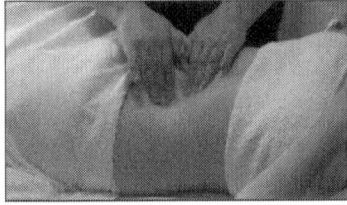

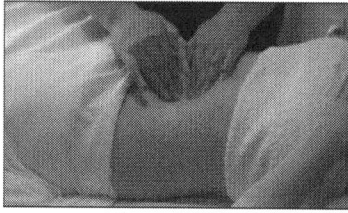

Neck

Start with head face up.

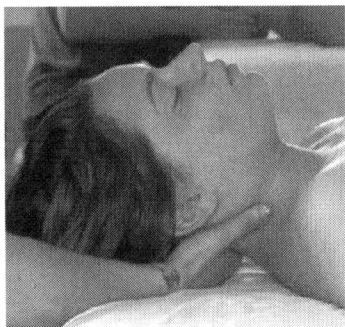

Turn the head to one side

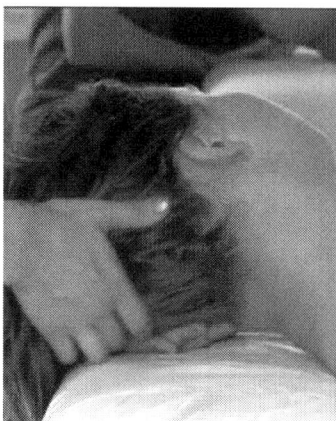

Knead with a single thumb down the side of the neck.

Knead lightly with your knuckles in a circular motion starting by the ear.

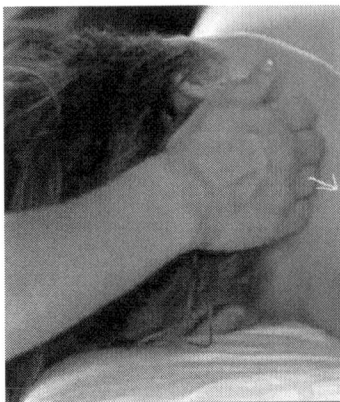

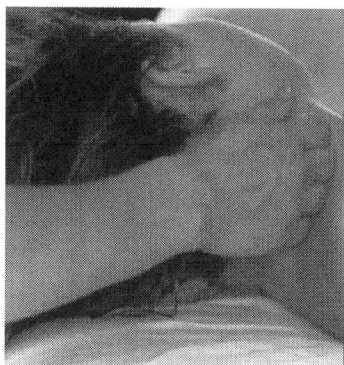

Head and Scalp

Slightly bend your fingers and make circles while keeping contact with clients /friends head

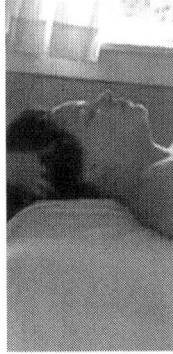

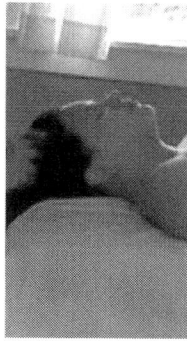

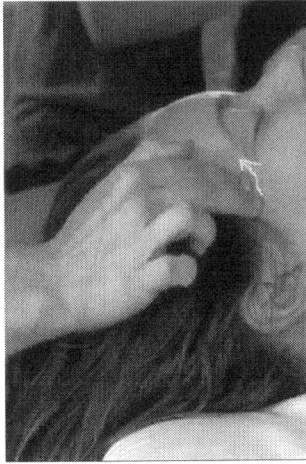

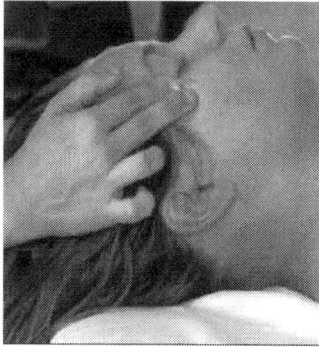

Hand

Alternate thumb kneading.

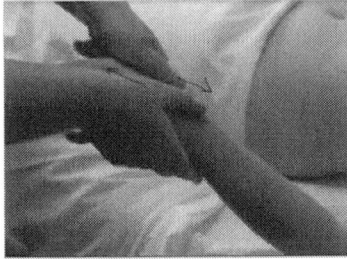

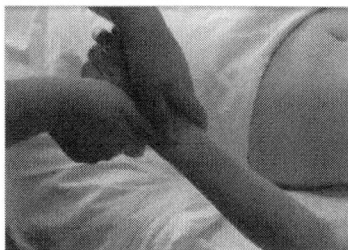

Forearm

Effleurage and thumb knead alternating hands moving between the wrist and elbow.

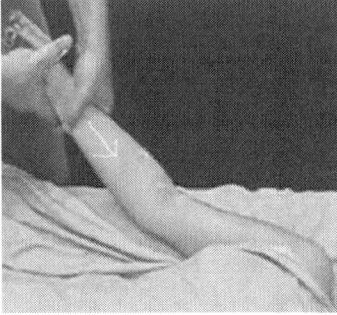

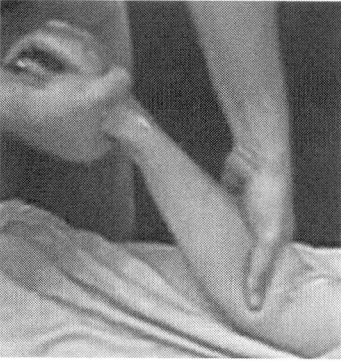

Arm

Finger Kneading:

Work your way to the shoulder then back to the elbow underneath the arm.

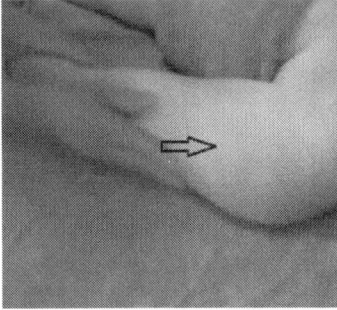

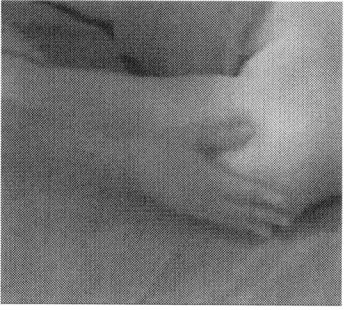

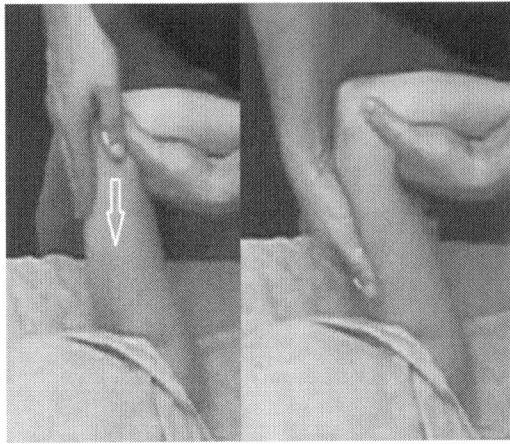

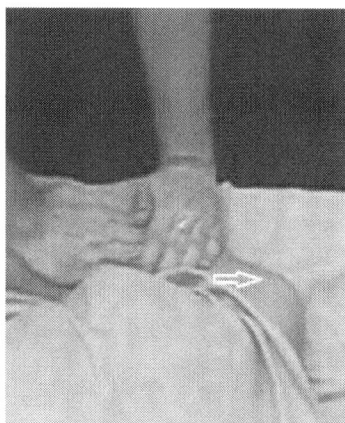

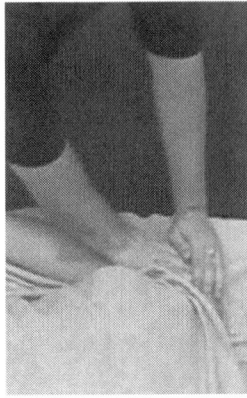

Quads /Anterior Thigh

Here you can finger knead, thumb knead and palmar knead

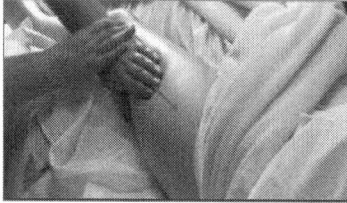

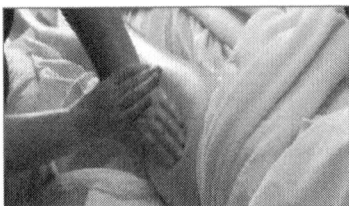

Groin

Alternate finger kneading with wringing

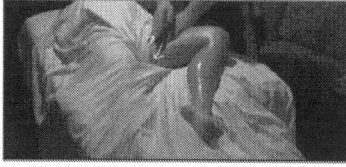

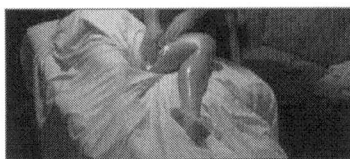

Glute / Buttocks

Circular motion with the palm and finger tips

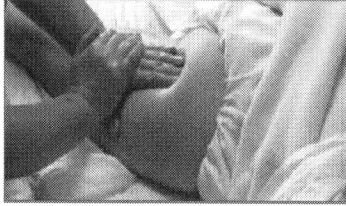

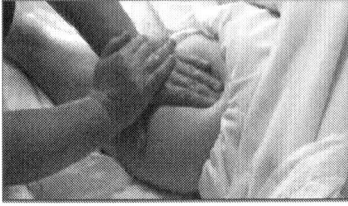

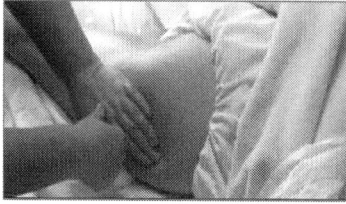

Hamstring / Posterior Thigh

Reinforced Palmar Kneading

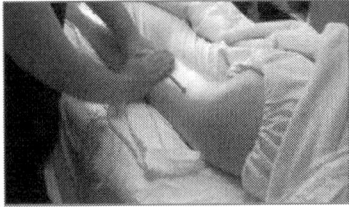

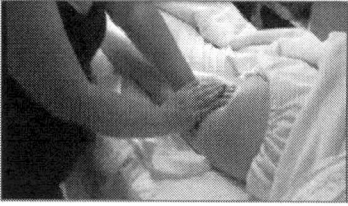

Calf Muscles

Thumb Kneading

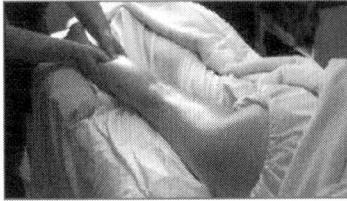

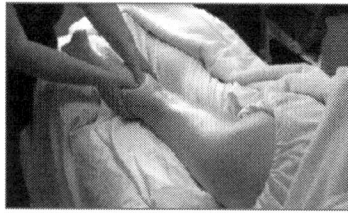

Foot

Palm and finger kneading

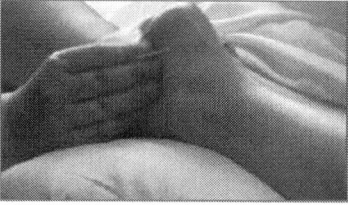

Full Body Massage

Here is a simple sequence that you can follow with your partner.

Face Down

1. Back: Effleurage, Finger Kneading, Thumb Kneading, Effleurage

2. Glutes: Effleurage, Reinforced Palmar Kneading, Pounding, Effleurage

3. Posterior Leg / Hamstring and Calves: Effleurage, Wringing, Thumb Kneading, Effleurage

4. Foot: Circular Motions

5. Finish: Effleurage from foot to glutes

Face Up

1. Anterior Legs: Effleurage, Finger kneading, Wringing, Effleurage

2. Arm / Forearm /Hand: Effleurage, Thumb Kneading, Finger Kneading, Wringing, Effleurage

3. Neck and Scalp: Circular Motions

Key Points to Remember

1. Start and finish with effleurage. It is a great stroke to help you apply oil and good to finish with a soothing effect.

2. Check your partner / client / friend to see if they have any allergies to nuts or oils.

3. Find a quiet area in your house or apartment.

4. Turn all cell phones off.

5. Give yourself and your partner / client / friend at least one hour without interruptions.

6. Find relaxing music.

7. Start with lighter pressure and gradually increase to stronger pressure.

8. Have your partner / client /friend remove any jewelry that may get in the way.

9. Enjoy yourself!

39161376R00053